The Universe

CW00428221

Contents

In this natural world, I find myself.
I find you.

Animal

An Unexpected Encounter

I saw a dead bird on the path,
lying there on grey asphalt.
I stopped with such a sudden start
that I almost turned inside myself.

Bird of Poetry

My wings may have been clipped
and I have lost more than a few
feathers in this fight for freedom
(you could call me the Balding Eagle).
But that doesn't matter;
for now, I am soaring high
across blue skies, wild and free,
the way birds are supposed to be.

Duality

Tiger at my back, camouflaged,
yet ready to pounce
on those who threaten
to take me down.

Owl in the sky overhead
watches me with her beady eyes,
soars with wings outspread,
hoots and sighs;

*"Remember, without trust,
you will never fly."*

And I try to hear
the words of the owl
over the tiger's growl,

and to know when
to let her pounce
and when to let her prowl.

Locusts

The trust that was forming
has been decimated
like crops in a plague of locusts;

bonds broken in the fracas.

Although the swarm has now departed,
my green land that once lay placid,
now lies bare and arid.

And I mourn the failed harvest.

Maybe I did not cultivate this earth
with the care and attention
that it deserved.

Maybe my fingers are not
so green after all
and this is all my fault.

Maybe this is me reaping
exactly what I have sown
or maybe the fault is not my own.

But in everything, a lesson learned.

At least now I know
the difference between
those who care and those who don't.

The Fish and the Sea

Who am I here?

I am a fish out of water
struggling to breathe.

I am the imposter
and I wonder how
I find myself to be here,
among those who are
so unlike me.

And can't they see?

I dream of the deep
blue sea that calls
my name, always.

And I so long to be
swimming through
the reefs, weightlessly,
with the currents
and the seaweed
all around me.

And with all those other fish
who understand me implicitly.

I am a fish and I need the sea.

Tigers and Sparrows

I used to be a wounded sparrow;
alone and vulnerable.
But I have flown so far
and my wings have grown
as I crossed the seas of blue
and deserts of sepia tones.
I grew the greatest, sharpest claws
and my little beak became
these fearsome teeth,
my feathers turned to fur...

And now I am a tiger,
alone and powerful
with glowing eyes of amber.

I wonder which one you prefer.

I am the tiger.

Vultures

I venture through the valley of the vultures
where all the dead things lie and rot.
Skeletons, old and new, in the sediment;
victims that time long forgot.
I stumble on the brink,
dying for a drink
from the River of Life
to push through this strife
and arrive at the river's edge,
far beyond the desert's glare.
But I am miles away from there
in the valley where the vultures fly.

Whale Song

This space where I am weightless; home to me.

Freedom.

Freedom to roam.

Freedom to be.

Arboreal

Blood Red Berries

In autumn, the streets are covered
with berries that have fallen from the trees.
Their little bodies lie lifeless
between the listless leaves.
Their berry blood stains the pavement
as I pass them laying there,
it spilled from those that were trampled
by feet that didn't care.

Deforestation

Ruminating the ruins of my life,
awaiting the next disaster that will fell me;
the disasters pending.
I see myself fall like a tree in a forest,
landing with a loud and brutal bang,
sending small creatures scurrying
and leaving a tree stump, broken,
where a glorious tree should stand.

Leave Me to Believe

Trees make me believe
in the air I breathe
and in the changing of the seasons
reflected in their leaves.

Trees make me believe
in the life that is all around me
like the birds that fly on high
who rest upon their branches.

Trees make me believe
in the ground on which I wander
and in this earthly mother
to whom we are all anchored.

Swing on the Willow Tree

Down by the willow tree, I find a place for me;
a place to be.

Swaying in the breeze with the flowers in harmony;
they bloom for me.

Swinging back and forth
Swinging back and forth
but not a child anymore

Seeking out butterflies, I offer them sorry sighs,
watch as they pass me by.

Wiping tear-stained eyes, look up to hazy skies,
starting to realise.

Swinging back and forth
Swinging back and forth
but not a child anymore

Cleansed by summer rains, washing away the stains,
washing away the pain.

Learning to start again, to enjoy making daisy chains
and singing one final refrain;

Swinging back and forth
Swinging back and forth
but not a child anymore
but not a child anymore

The Furies

You think that you can shake me?
Please!
I have faced the furies of storms.
I laugh in the face of your breeze.

The Tree in Me

A love that I could not foresee
has all but taken over me.
It planted roots, became a tree
now it stands strong, now it stands free.

The Universe Sends Me Blossoms

Blossoms on the wind remind
me that time is fleeting;
that I cannot hold on to them or you.
In this duo where everything said
seems to undo the love, the affection.
And I cannot change you and
should not want to...
so I will heed the warnings
of a universe in motion,
telling me,
"No, this is not the way to go."

Under Giant Trees

Under giant trees, I wander
and I ponder as I wander
at all of these epiphanies
encountered
whilst walking
under giant trees.

Under giant trees, I wander
and I ponder as I wander
at all of these prophecies
whispered to me
whilst walking
under giant trees.

I wander in good company,
walking under giant trees.

Celestial

Beacon

A corridor of light stretches across
the dark ocean, still but rippling.

And I am rowing, tirelessly,
along the passageway.

Losing sleep because this
means everything to me.

Refusing to lose focus
in the darkness.

I know where I am going
and what I am out to find.

Her face gazes down on me,
but yours is on my mind.

Cosmic Connection

What is this connection
between us?
This invisible bond,
gravitational pull?

Planetary bodies orbiting
in the darkness,
finding moments of alignment
in the void of it all.

Through dust clouds,
asteroids and magnetic fields,
and millions of light years,
I can feel you still.

Were we once one?
Were we cut from the same core?

Why is it that when I look
into your eyes,
I see the reflection
of my own soul?

Eclipsed

Eclipses are momentary,
everything is in motion.

We forget this sometimes
with our human eyes
and our human minds
and our human perception
of the passage of time.

We are particles of stardust
in a vast cosmos;
we are nothing
short of miraculous.

This universe;
four billion years
in the making,
won't stop for us.

One day, the sun will die;
she will expand and eat us alive.
I'm hoping we don't destroy
ourselves in the meantime.

Reflections

I found myself by the lakeside,
stopped and stared,
basking in the light of a
thousand stars that glittered,
reflected in the water.

The stars were watching, wide-awake,
sat blinking and twinkling
from their distant lake,
began to whisper, murmur,
"Come here. Come and take a peek."

*I wished I could but didn't want
to spoil the view.*

But I tiptoed closer to the water
and saw the appearance of
my contours, my features blurred,
and I was no longer a human creature
but had transformed into a star.

They chuckled and winked at me,
*"Now you can see what we can see.
Your human eyes are not as heavenly
but you are so much more than
you perceive yourself to be."*

Supernova

I wish that our love had died
like some stars do;
in a glorious supernova.
Putting on one final dazzling display
for the universe,
not content to go out any other way.
Our love did not die a dazzling death.
It simply shrunk and fizzled away.

Waxing, Waning

Sit with me a while, I will let you shine
and ask for nothing more
for you owe me nothing.
Well! I would ask, on second thought,
for one thing; can I swim
to your silver shores?

Through the darkest, deepest, endless sea
forged in a time before time was time.
To meet you, face of the night,
constant comfort and solace.

To pass beyond countless constellations
of twinkling stars, forever blinking,
that say, *"not far, keep swimming"*
towards your bright light
which breaks the night and
calms my soul.

We Are Sailors and Astronauts

Rain rivers for me, a thousand raindrops
leading me to the sea to sail away with you.

Sailing across the open waters, the endless blue...

Visiting vibrant harbours and exotic ports,
sailing to lonely islands and distant shores.

Exploring all there is to explore and more...

Reaching the horizon and daring to go beyond
the meridian and all those imaginary boundaries.

Exchanging our seas for galaxies...

Astral bodies in distant oceans wait for us to arrive,
preparing displays of shooting stars for our eyes.

Breathless in the timelessness, you and I...

Marvelling at black holes and the Rings of Saturn,
knowing that our journey has just begun.

Knowing that you are my stars, my moon, my sun...

Yūgen*

I feel like that a lot;
like a tiny dot
in the vast cosmos.
Nothing really.
Sometimes I wish
I could reach out
and touch its black waters,
watch the ripples flow
through space and time.
But I cannot.
But I cannot.

*幽玄 / ゆうげん

Elemental

Dancing

These sunsets set my soul on fire...
and I will dance across pink skies forever
and bounce across grey clouds
and settle in the setting sun.
I'm never coming down!

Dust Clouds

I always was two steps
behind you, losing time,
I think I liked it that way;
distant and solitary.
Never quite ready
to hand over my soul or
to give you much of me at all.

And you always thought I was
the one chasing you
but that wasn't quite true...
I was dreaming of other lives
and of being another's wife
and it was never your face
that I saw in the night.

It was never quite right.
So I leave you for the last time;
I leave you behind.
Look back, it is not me
you will find, I am not there.
I have left you with nothing
but the dust clouds in the air.

I argue with clouds

Road empty of cars, sky full of grey clouds;
dark and heavy, waiting to burst perhaps.

And I tell them, if you're going to rain then rain heavy.

Rain so that the sky rips open with thunder.

Let the lightening reach down and electrify me.

Rain so that I can feel it trickling
on my skin, permeating
the layers and organs
that lie within.

Because if you're not going to revive me,
if you're not going to shock and terrify me,
if you're not going to rain heavy then
just go away and leave me to my day...

because what I feel, I feel completely.

Raindrops

A lake alive with raindrops causing ripples.
They appear and then disappear;
raindrops, ripples.
Raindrops rest on branches bare from winter
and her bitter cold.
Now they stand embellished with dewy drops.
Raindrops play a quiet melody on my umbrella
reminding me; *it's still raining*.
The distance; a hazy grey.
A watercolour day.

Testament

I once saw a rainbow appear;
a great arc in the sky,
a gateway to who knows where.

I watched until she disappeared,
the hands of a god erased her,
the only hands that dared.

I stood mesmerized at the sight

and hoped with a heart sincere
that others too have witnessed the wonder
of watching a rainbow appear and then disappear.

The Path Ahead is Green

Follow the trails, the trees and all those
paths covered in leaves.

Follow the melodies of all those
birds singing to me.

Follow the scent of flowers that bloom
in all those eye-catching colours.

Follow the streams full of fish and all
their piscine dreams.

Follow mountain tops tipped in white and
all those stars shining at night.

Follow the footsteps in the desert
of all those fearless explorers.

Follow the sunrise and follow her
until she sets before your eyes.

With every footstep forward I find,
it is the grey path I leave behind.

Volcanic

I worry about these things that
inspire this quiet rebellion within me;
I worry about that impending eruption
plunging lives into ruin and anarchy.

And I feel the blood boiling
in my veins; restless, pressure building
like the molten magma through
underground vents rising;

the chaos beneath the surface calm.

I worry about these things that
trigger the subtle tremors within,
seismic changes threatening
bedlam and the end of all things.

One day you may see me exploding
and spewing forth great ash clouds
and pyroclastic fragments;
suffocating and sky-darkening.

And I will awaken in the aftermath,
comprehending the destruction
that I have left; the hell of it
and a lava trail of regrets.

Could I contain such violence?

The volcano rumbles and I tremble.

Was I always so blue?

It's like walking on a sunny day
and feeling nothing but the rain
and all of those dark, dark clouds
bearing down.

Floral

Dandelions

Tear apart the pieces of me,
I offer them to you.
I embrace this opportunity
to unravel, to undo.

Tear apart the pieces of me,
scatter my seeds to sow.
I embrace this opportunity
to relinquish, to let go.

Tear apart the pieces of me,
watch them flutter free
like the pappus of dandelions
dancing in the breeze.

Floral Palette

Like flowers in nature,
we are humans of a
thousand different colours,
surrounded by
seas of blue
and forests of green.

Seasons march past us
and we witness the
the changing of our leaves.

All of those petals fallen;

all that we are
and all that we
have ever been.

We wait for the blossoming;

all of these shades of you
and these shades of me
just waiting to be seen.

Lily and the Moon

I will water you with
waterfalls of love
and watch you bloom,
not just for the shining sun
but for the silver moon
and her stars above.

Moonflowers

Some flowers only bloom at night,
awakened by the pale moonlight.

Mourning the Passing of my Flowers and my Colours

I dress in black;
all of my flowers have died,
all my roses, all my daffodils
and I face this world unfilled.

I am in mourning,
trying to reassemble them;
their petals, their little leaves,
but I am unsuccessful.

I lament;
they have withered and perished;
with them, my colours have faded,
and they have left me achromatic.

My Heart in a Flower

You are my favourite little thing;
my heart in a flower
that grows and blossoms every day
and takes my breath away.

I will carry you with me
in a special bouquet
and tend to you
in the night and in the day.

And I will be whatever
you need me to be,
just say the word.
You are what I call *love*.

Thorn in my Side

He did not bring me roses
instead he left me
on the doorstep,
in the darkness.

There are many things
that I can forgive,
that I can forget
but this is not one of them.

Wildflowers

My stems have been severed,
they tore me from this earth
to stand me in a vase of water
with artificial flower feed.

They took my happiness from me.

This is *not* where wildflowers are
supposed to be.

Hadal

Death is a Distant Shore or the Ocean Floor

Swimming towards a shore
that I cannot see but
must ultimately reach
one day.

Swimming and tiring with every
movement forward and
wondering if I should relinquish
and allow myself to sink.

Going under and leaving nothing
but a trail of bubbles
on the surface water
and they too will disappear.

And what would it be to sink?

To sink and see a pod of orcas chasing krill.

To sink further still.

To sink and watch seashores darting in and out of coral.

To continue the descent past
all of these strange creatures,
all weird and wonderful and bioluminescent,
lights in the deepest darkness.

They look at me,
"Strange being, you don't belong here.
Go back up to the surface before you run out of air."

Harbours

You are my harbour.
You are my safe haven,
the place where I can
lay my anchor.

You are my shelter
from the storms
that threaten to
shake me to my core.

You are my phare.
You are my beacon
of hope in the darkness
that I cannot ignore.

And as I sail to distant shores
and across the endless blue,
just know that I am always
making my way home to you.

You are my harbour.

Kraken

Threatened by the kraken,
threatens to crack me open
and tear me limb from limb;

succeeding.

Watches, triumphant, as all
of my secrets spill from me
into saline solution.

Gathers them up like treasure
with his many tentacles,
far-reaching.

Hide them in a treasure chest.

Promise to protect them forever
now that you have pried them
from my chest.

Keep them hidden in these depths.

Swim away through the endless seas,
swim away with all my mysteries
and please try to be
more forgiving of them

than I could ever be.

Pirates of Old

I plunder these caves;
like pirates of old
in search of treasure and gold,
and that which I will never find,
fruitless in my quest.
Alone on this cove,
as I should have foretold,
these pirates of old
have already emptied this trove
and I find a vacant treasure chest and
a shipwreck surrounded by sea shells.
These sea shells, now hollow and void,
once home to life,
beckon me with the false call
of a distant sea;
an echo from a time long gone,
remnants of a distant dream almost forgotten.
I should sail to another shore
where I may find treasure galore
but the risk is high and the journey long
and I fear that I will find myself, instead,
on the sea floor where I will be doomed to rest
forever more with the pirates of old.

~~Some Improvement Required~~
She Conquered Poseidon for Me

Thank you for this label, I will try to embrace it
as I wish you well on your power trip.
But you should know, before you go, that
it is the **rebel** you forced me to acknowledge.

She was screaming whilst I was silent.
She was dreaming whilst I was blinded.

I held her under great seas of water
but even they could not contain her;
her spirit never faltered.

She overflowed against repression,
bursting free in a grand outpouring;
an unholy uprising.

Falling to my knees, I witnessed
her rising with Poseidon's trident,
knowing in that moment, that she
alone was worthy of my respect.

And with her ascension came
the liberation from years of tension
that I had been holding within.

She placed a shell over my heart,
triumphant, and whispered,
"We will never be apart.
This is the armour that we share
now that we are one and the same thing."

Shells

She is a shell.
Something used to dwell
within; a beautiful being,
but that was long ago
and now she's void and hollow.

I hold her to my ear
and try to hear
the echoes of the ocean;
the songs I've heard before
but I can't hear them anymore.

I place her gently on the sand,
I have to leave her on this shore.
In an ocean of many echoes,
I try to hold on to yours.

The Sea Mist

So much that I can't remember,
I think that the anchor has slipped
and I have set off adrift,
floating through the gaps
and the crevices
way beyond my destination.

I lose myself to the sea mist.

I can no longer see the horizon
as I sail blindly in the
company of sirens
wailing, wily witches
willing to lead me astray.
Maybe I should follow them.

What is life but an adventure anyway?

The ships that sail the seas...

All those seas I've sailed.
All those ships I've passed in the night.
All those ships I've lost to storms.
All those sailors taken by the sirens and their songs.
All those seabirds squawking overhead.
All those sharks circling below.
All those swells I've navigated,
all those streams and undertows.
All those shores I've never reached.
All those shores I never will.
Captain of this ship, across these seas I sail.

Musical

Alien

Voices in the day and in the night,
voices in the chorus, those voices rising.
I wish I knew the song
that they are singing.
Is this what it means to be *alien*?

-less

It is a tragedy
when poets abandon their pens,
when artists put down their brushes
and singers lose their voices.
The heart breaks.
The soul cries.
We rot and we putrefy.
We shrivel and darken
and wither into oblivion.

Listen

There are strange songs
that I can hear from my window,
in the days and in the nights.
They tell me about all these other lives
taking place at my sides
and far away on distant shores.
I try to listen but they are only echoes.

Maestro

I must dust off my heart strings
to allow that budding musician
the chance to play a subtle melody;
one that could fill this empty
chamber with the echoes
of a most brilliant vibrato
that pulsates and resonates
through my veins and to my core.
For I have forgotten how to feel
such vibrations in my being.
So play! Play now and play on
and play those magical chords
that cut through the cacophony;
the discord that surrounds me,
to leave my soul in harmony.

Replenish

I am going to compose
a thousand songs
to fill the empty
spaces in my lungs
and the blank pages
of my heart.

I am going to fill
huge stadiums
with people
and put on for them
the most wonderful
shows and spectacles.

All singing, all dancing

And I will feel it all again;
The hope
The joy
The love
The inspiration

Those fleeting feelings,
too easily depleted by
the trials and tribulations
and problems of life
that leave us broken,
empty and numb.

Those fleeting feelings,
I will replenish them.

Soul Song

I heard you all along,
little starling sings my song.
I heard you in the distance
and even in the darkness.
I heard you through the maelstrom
and even through the madness.
When my eyes could not find you
and my soul was steeped in sadness,
I heard you all along,
little starling sings my song.

The sea sings the softest songs

I can hear her calling me;
the deep, blue, endless sea.
She sends her winds to embrace me,
they caress my skin and stroke my hair
and pull me closer. Closer to her
and to her sandy shores;
the warmth, the waves.
I'm coming.
I'm coming back to you.
Wait for me...

The Tango between Pleasure and Pain

I watch it unravelling, spine tingling;
the tango between pleasure and pain.
Their footsteps dancing across
the contours of my body
like fingers scratching, caressing.

Perfect partners, feet tapping,
tension mounting, swirling
and I hear the notes from
the violins rising; their strings
screeching, haunting.

I'm caught in the power play
between pleasure and pain.
They sway and I feel everything.

Chaos choreographed to perfection;
the aching, the longing,
hearts beating and breaking.
Bodies in frenzied motions
throwing caution to the wind...

Me pierdo en los pasos.
Me rindo al ritmo.
Me olvido en el juego.
Espero el daño.
Lo entiendo todo.
Bailo el tango entre el placer y el dolor.

Nocturnal

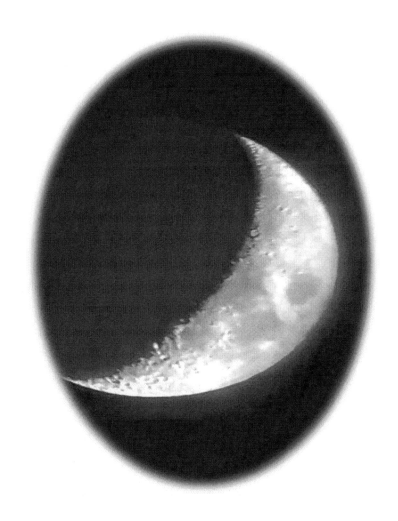

Between Breadcrumbs and Beasts

Cold night, frost forming,
darkness settles in
as I trample the skeletons
of all these dead leaves
and these frozen things.

Seeking breadcrumbs
of hope I'm hoping
someone left for me,
for when the night comes
I cannot see any light
between these trees.

And I don't know
what is stalking me
from the shadows
but I feel it watching with
those nocturnal eyes that glow.

I would never let it show
but these dark woods,
they scare me so,
they put the fear into my bones.
I tiptoe as I go, hiding
the terror in my soul.

Dark Dragon

I have carried you on my back for so long.
There were times when I thought
that you had left me, taken flight,
but I was wrong.
The fire you set, it flickers on
and it takes but an ember
to set my entire brain aflame
and, once again, I must be strong.
Your appearance was not and
has never been invited.
And I have sought to destroy you
several times, quite rightly!
But you have proven to be a mighty opponent;
an enemy so engrained in me
that I once wondered if
killing you meant killing me.
No! I know better.
This fight is long and exhausting
but my fate is not to be
a pile of ashes of your making.

Don't Scratch the Surface

There is a depression that lies
beneath the surface,
when you are seconds away
from doing yourself
some serious damage.
I'm there, trying not to scratch.
Don't break the skin.
Don't let the darkness in.

So dark the night...

The night reaches out
sending her shadows
in mysterious shapes,
past minds deep in sleep,
deep in dreamscapes.

The mind's eye wanders
and conjures terrible creations;
meaningful and meaningless
all at once.

Full of familiar places never visited
and familiar faces never seen;
the land of dreams
beyond that of slumber.

As paralyzed bodies lie
alone in the darkness,
alone in the night,
the night song rises
and whispers *"sleep tight."*

The Dark Arts that Illuminate My Heart

I am the sorceress standing at my cauldron,
all kinds of concoctions and potions boiling,
bubbling and brewing.

Dried herbs hanging from the ceiling
beside shrunken skulls; unholy offerings
to the ancient deities I am conjuring.

Mixing tinctures and elixirs to heal
the wounds scratched into my soul
by the werewolves and hounds of Hell.

Casting circles and chanting rituals,
clutching my protective symbols
and creeping closer to the threshold.

This is my alchemy.
This is my supernatural symphony.
This is me reaching into the darkness.
This is her pulling back at me.

Tempting me to come in.
Tempting me to be more trusting.
Tempting me to relinquish, *give in*;
all without seeing what lies within.

Me, faltering on the rim, hearing
those wise ravens whispering,
"Love can be a dark thing
but there is also light within."

These Thoughts

These thoughts dash from the darkness and steal my slumber.
Like spiders from corners creep, they disturb my sleep and my
mind wanders.
They linger all around my bed and in my head
and talk to me of woe and dread.
Entangled in their woven web, as reason ebbs
and flows, and the terror grows.
I lie ensnared and cry in despair as I search
the gloom for a glint, a glimmer
of light, of hope, a subtle shimmer,
of something, of anything
to which I can tether.
Please be there.

Tiptoe through Shadows

I am so drawn to the darkness
and all those dark creatures
that dwell within
but I know when I can enter it
and when to keep my distance.

You are not alone in the night

There are lights in the night;
beacons to guide us home
or, at least, somewhere safe,
somewhere warm.

Follow them...

Rhetorical

I Cannot Piece Them Together

To those undone, who lie in fragments,
I do apologise. For, you see,
I cannot remember
what you were meant to be,
what you were meant to say.

Too much time and space
has passed between us
and my heart has not grown fonder
but has grown forgetful.

And so you are lost to the firmament
of a foggy memory that can't recall
what you were meant to say,
what you were meant to be.

And I fear that you are doomed
to rest there for all eternity.

All these lost elements of me…

Love's Labour

My words; not just ink on paper
but my love, my days' labour
which allow me to deliver
speckles of my soul;
the elements of me.
My life. My poetry.

Love Stories

I wish that someone would
look at me that way;
with the love of a thousand
love stories in their eyes.

Parapraxis

It's ok, I know.
I know that the things
we say in anger are often
tinged with truth.

Hints of honesty and ruthlessness
that slip through when
we let down our defences,
when our mind is a little
distracted.

Soliloquy

You never fought my departure;
no protest from you,
so I can't help but wonder
if you wanted it too.

The Language of Lovers

The hand that reaches out
to touch the arm of their lover.
Breaking any void between them
and acting as a reminder
to say, "*I love you.*
You are mine and I am yours,
and we are bound together
by a chemistry that cannot
be quantified or measured.
For we are the lovers".

The Poetry in Flaws and Fallacies

Sometimes I put words together
in the wrong order and a poem
is born.

And I realise that it would not
exist at all if I was right
all the time.

So I suggest that we seek to find
the poetry hiding in our
flaws and fallacies.

There is Beauty in the Beastly

My poetry may be ghastly,
rough around the edges,
even ugly but it is a
reflection of me
and of all that I see.

To write it is to hold it,
to embrace it and all the
pain, the agony, the beauty, the beastly.

To know it.
To feel it.
To look it in the eye
and say, *"I saw you today
and I will see you again tomorrow"*.

Sentimental

Always Alone

I would prefer to say that
I'll be going back to solitude
but, the truth is that,
with you, I never left it.
Maybe that's the reason
why I am not feeling sorrow
now but am feeling
disappointment.

Driftwood

All those days when
the pain was too much
to articulate.

And all those days when
I missed you too much
to say.

And all those days when
my love drifted too far
away.

I was drifting away.
I drifted away.

Housewarming Gift

I gave you a picture frame
for your new home,
the space that you share with her.

And we can engage in
a platonic embrace,
there are no romantic feelings here.

And we can catch up
and talk about work,
grab some drinks and dinner.

And I will not take things
out of context or look for a
subtext that does not exist.

But there will come a time when
I can no longer look into your eyes
and hide these sentiments inside.

So forgive me; I will push you away.
Create a little more space,
that's what I do.

Because I don't know
how to feel these feelings
for you

and I have resolved never
to break a happy home
in two.

Incendiary

Swirling streams of sultry smoke
scenting everything.
I allow myself to breathe it in;
temporary indulgence.
Evading hands that wrongly
reached out to touch; better that way,
as this is illusionary, this is reverie.

Another dream just out of reach...

But I let the scent linger
on my hair and on my clothing,
knowing that I will pay for this concession.
Letting it penetrate the skin,
infuse my internal organs and
infiltrate the walls of my heart, beating.
Give into it, just for a little bit.

Bite my lip...

Re-establish my defences,
wash soot stains from fingertips,
hide the evidence, put away the matches.
Remove all of my flammable possessions
and spend today hoping
that I don't see you tomorrow
and wishing that I do.

Incendiary; these flames burning for you...

It hurts but I must do this...

I could not say that, with you,
my fire died but
it certainly diminished.
And all around me,
these other fires started
that I had to extinguish.
And although I extinguished
you in the process
and burned my fingers
in the anguish,
I brought myself
back into balance and,
this, I do not regret.

Shades of Me

I cannot guarantee that all these shades of me
won't fade away to grey someday.

And when I come to be a silhouette of me
will you stay with me that way?

And as the colours run and the lines begin to blur
will you see the image of me beneath?

And if I'm lost to time, would you seek to find
the traces of me that I leave behind...

for you?

Solid Gold

I see the golden sunrise
and feel the rays of a thousand
sunbeams warming my eyes
and dancing across my skin;

embracing
me
inviting them in;

sunbeams seeping into every
fibre of my being
all fiery and alive,
all warm and glowing.

Life with you is golden.

To Drown

I would dive into those eyes;
cool, blue pools, inviting.
From there, I would swim
and follow rivers of veins
to your soul; an ocean,
glistening.
You will find me there,
drowning.

Spiritual

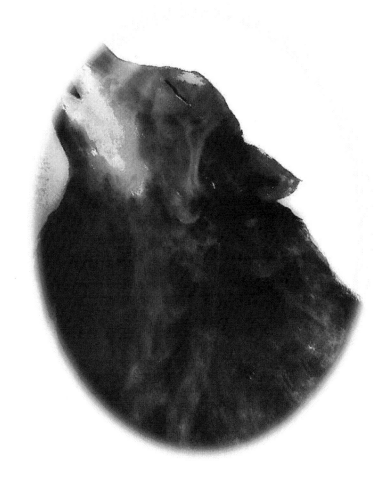

Achromatic

I am grey.
I dive into these colours
to become colourful
but they wash off
as I leave this pool
and I am grey still.

Awaken

Sun rising over sea and mountains
and in my eyes.

Green things awakening, stirring,
coming back to life.

Finding stillness in the spaces between
the bees and butterflies.

Sunlight on skin is warming,
letting softness flow back in.

And I hold on to this sensation
that restores me to my being

and helps me breathe again.

Cogs

I am the faulty
cog in the machine;
jarring sometimes to
cause a little chaos or
some much needed disruption,
stuck between boredom
and rebellion in this land
I call *"Rebeldom"*.

I look at these other cogs
around me, they are
grey and weary.
Caught up in the motion,
never stopping, never thinking
as they go round and round
for someone else's dream,
for someone else's vision.

I'd rather stand alone and power my own
than be a cog in this machine.

I wish I were an island...

Maybe we unleash this chaos
just to feel something.
All too quickly forgetting
that all of our actions
have repercussions
on so many other beings.

Ice Fortress

Frost lingers in shaded spaces
out of bright sunlight;
all of those deep recesses
out there and in here,
suffering from frostbite.

I wander past icicles
and sharp edges,
glistening beautifully
whilst threatening to
impale me.

I wasn't always so cold.

I tiptoe into sunbeams sneaking
through the skeletons of trees,
feeling the thawing
of that ice fortress;
surrendering into streams.

I follow them;
the trickling droplets
forming waterfalls within,
the waters warming.
Should I just jump in?

Sensing the tingling
in frozen regions that
have forgotten sensation;
the burning but passing pain.
The ice fortress has fallen.

Ravenous

Why still this emptiness inside me
that plagues and haunts me?

Did I not fill you with somethings
and everythings and anythings
and all these trivial things
that you demanded of me?

And still you stare me down,
glaring and gaping.
And a little bit of my soul is breaking.
Always breaking.

I feel tired and empty.
These things that I do in life,
they don't fulfil me.
Why don't they fulfil me?

And even with you by my side,
in the day and in the night,
I feel it still, alive and breathing;
the lacking.

This void, this hole within my soul,
always yearning. Hungry and starving.

And I cannot feed it or put my finger
on what is missing. *What am I missing?*

Why still this emptiness inside me?

Wolves

I will not tame the wild wolves of my nature.
With them, I will run free.

I will hear their primal howl, the call of the wild,
they call to me.

I will follow paw prints in the snow,
they left for me.

I will find my way back to my pack,
they wait for me.

I will embrace them, blood-stained fangs
and all.

I will walk with them under moons,
crescent and full.

I will find my origins in this fertile land
we cross.

Together we will hunt and stalk the freedoms
I have lost.

I will not tame the wild wolves of my nature.
With them, I will run free.

For freedom is innate in all wild things
and wild I will be.

Yearning

The soul sighs...she is empty.
In her eyes are the memories of tears
that now refuse to cry.

Temporal

Don't Blink

I can hear it in my ear...

the incessant clanging of the clock.
It chimes and strikes and ticks and tocks
and I am hypersensitive to its every assault.

I count my life in years and months
and days and minutes and all those speedy
seconds that march on by without my permission.

And I have reached the dreaded realisation
that I will never have quite enough.

Formation

Trickles of truth shape me
like the trickling streams that
have spent centuries
carving out rocks and mountains,
meticulously.
I don't have enough time.
I don't have centuries.

In the chrysalis, waiting for the moment

We emerge from our chrysalis as butterflies,
breaking the stasis, having entered
as caterpillars ready to die,
finding, instead, life and reincarnation.

You were always a butterfly within
waiting for the chance, the moment
to grow those wonderful wings,
to land on flowers and colourful things

and fly...

It is Time

A solitary autumn leaf falls before me;
golden in the green grass,
landing with the smallest of noises;
a tiny, tiny thud.

As if she had finally given up
holding on to her branch,
deciding, now, to let go and
to be swept along by autumn.

As if she had any other choice.

Quicksand

I know that all of these moments
are like quicksand in my hands.
And I lament all of those grains that pass
too quickly for my hands to catch;
the ones that slip between the cracks,
the ones I'm never getting back.

They form a desert at my feet.

Sometimes

Sometimes I see butterflies
flying by and I am reminded
of the fluidity of time;

that everything changes
and we must be dynamic
as the world around us rearranges.

We adapt or die and leave behind
those who are static,
those stuck in stone,
those stuck in time.

The Arrival of Spring

Winter is finally letting go
and spring is skipping in.
Armies of daffodils invading
green spaces but I barely
noticed them arrive.

Bright sun on crisp days
assaults my eyes
but that's alright;
for her warm rays
open doors in my soul
that I had closed
against winter's cold.

Woven, Unwoven

As the web of time unwinds
and it leaves me far behind,
I do not fear some grand design
or fateful ploy.
For nothing more
beyond these shores
does wait for me.
This is do believe.
That death is resolute, absolute
for all things that live and breathe.
And to know that those I love
will go on and live beyond
the days that I will live to see -
those days gifted to me –
is all the peace I will ever need
and the legacy I weave.

Universal

All I Need

What I need is for my perception of what I need to be challenged.
What I need is to see that excess is neither success nor happiness.
What I need is to break down doors that others have closed.
What I need is to embrace all that waits to be known.
What I need is to stare evil in the face and to fight it with kindness.
What I need is to dismantle all that I have been shown.
What I need is to balance the light with the darkness.
What I need is to appreciate all these seeds that I have sown.
What I need is to have those that I love around me.
What I need is to know that this is all I need.

This is all I need.

Fireworks

All of those moments of your life
that seemed insignificant, trivial,
they were not nothing.
They were something
and some of them were
decisions in disguise.

They were the moments
that led you to this
great explosion;

to the fireworks of your life.

Your graduation?
Your wedding day?
Your sobriety?
The birth of your first creation?

Those little moments dance in celebration;
without them your life would not be
the fireworks that you now see.

Inspired

And so I see more clearly now
those who offer inspiration
and those who drain it.

And those that I must
seek out who do not
seek to tame it.

And those that light a
flame in you so bright
you can't contain it.

And those that spark a
feeling in you so rare
you cannot name it.

And those that offer
a hand in the darkness
so you can take it.

You are the reason that I am here.
You are the reason that I made it.

Miracles and Monsters

Our creations are often monstrous beings
that rise up to bring us down.

Others are our salvation,
sent to save us when we drown.

Parachutes

I have leapt from the plane;
I have taken a leap of faith.

What is it I believe in again?

Free falling through blue skies,
I can barely open my eyes.

I clutch my parachute tightly.

Does that defeat the purpose?
I cling to it, regardless.

Feeling the rush of adrenalin
but always fearing the hard landing.

Wondering if something will catch me
in the end and if I will find my safety net.

Or is it the hard surface that awaits?

Surfacing

Sometimes you have to go down
to come up, to resurface,
coughing and spluttering,
turmoil and anguish vanquished.
It can seem counterintuitive but
you have to go with it and trust
that when you rise on the other side,
you'll be wiser, stronger and you'll know
that, next time, you can hold your
breath that little bit longer.

The Wall

There is but one thing that I have truly mastered
and I did it without much thinking or much effort;
I built a wall around me to find comfort
and to stop myself from ever getting hurt.

And now within this immense construction,
I reach a sad and frightening conclusion,
that this greatest conquest of my doing
will be my greatest regret and undoing.

Because I cannot see beyond these walls
that I have built so strong and tall.

Within the safety of this cell, I come to see
that I have traded liberty for security,

and blocked out all the light
that could have reached me,

and blocked out all the loves
that could have loved me.

I did not build a wall at all;
I built a prison for my soul.

Walking, Watching, Waiting

Walking, alone, at night through torrential rain,
street lights in the dark; blurry beacons
guiding me home again.

Watching, alone, birds dancing in unison
through Venetian skies; an effortless perfection
unfolding just for my eyes.

Waiting, alone, outside shop windows and cafes
for friends and lovers; on journeys delayed,
people watching, staring into space.

Walking, watching, waiting.
Life on pause, life in motion.

Visceral

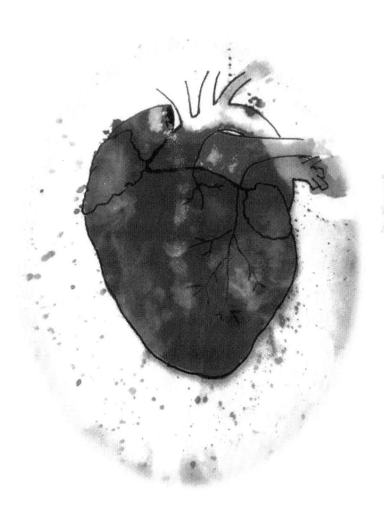

Chemical Bonds

This visceral inclination pulls
me back to you;
the mind moves forward but
the body lingers.
I see your face in the faces of
strangers in the crowd,
my eyes try to seek you out.
But I cannot move backwards now
so I keep my distance and
leave a little bit extra space
between us.

Heavy Heart

Medusa, do not look at me!
For my heart is already made of stone
and I do not think I could carry on
if the rest of me was entombed.

I See

To see this world in its entirety;
the good, the bad,
the beautiful, the ugly,
is a gift, not to be taken
for granted or taken lightly.

Inhalation

I opened up my heart and
a thousand words spilled out
in quiet jubilation.

They pooled around my feet
and began to submerge me
in rising inspiration.

I opened up my mouth
and began to find that
after years of suffocation,
I'm finally inhaling.
I'm finally inhaling.

Note to Self

I suffer from such forgetfulness,
forgetting all of those reasons
why I left in the first place.

I have to remind myself,

*"You are not by his side
because you chose not
to occupy that space."*

Self-preservation

My Heart sings at the top of her lungs
and my Head tells her to calm down,
lower the volume so that we can
think for a moment
but she's having none of it.

My Head reminds her that to us
this is the great unknown
and that we don't want to
lose ourselves to the delirium
that comes when love knocks on the door.

And that we don't wear
the shawl of envy very well;
it doesn't complement our skin tone
and neither do obsession or yearning
or that grey shade of forlorn.

And our Eyes were so tired
after all you made them suffer;
all those hours of lost slumber
that no amount of coffee
or mascara could cover.

And our Hands got so bloody
mending all your broken shards.
I'm sorry, Heart, but
we *all* almost died the
last time you fell apart.

Thirst

Maybe I have travelled too far
down this path to turn back.
Over my shoulder, I see
the hot air rising; a sandy mirage
and nothing but a blur of the days
that have passed.

Everything around me is parched
but I cannot afford to weep
for this scorched earth.

My compass is faulty and
I have lost my bearings in
the sameness of the desert
and her merciless sandstorms.

And blue skies above are deceptive,
unwilling to reveal what lies
ahead in any direction.
Do you wish to see me fail?

Still, I search for an oasis
knowing only too well
that straying from the right path
would be to perish.
The desert is cold-hearted.
She is brutal and callous.

Her winds torment and whisper,
*"Keep going, you may yet find water
if the thirst doesn't kill you first."*

Unyielding

I offer an ode to this body
which, despite its imperfections,
houses my soul with a loyalty,
unyielding.

Acknowledgements

I'm not sure what brought you on this journey,
perhaps it was passion, chance or curiosity,
but I thank you for taking it with me and
for exploring my art and my poetry.

I would like to extend my gratitude to Eyewear Publishing Ltd © for recognising my work and for featuring my poem, *The ships that sail the seas,* in their Best New British and Irish Poets anthology of 2019 – 2020.

A special thanks to the friends and family who have lent their support, creativity and artistic eyes to the creation and publication of this collection.

About the Author

Scottish poet, SA Willis, started writing poetry in her childhood; a passion which she nurtured by studying languages and literature at the University of Edinburgh. A lover of nature and travel, her work is frequently inspired by the natural world and the mysteries it contains.

Printed in Poland
by Amazon Fulfillment
Poland Sp. z o.o., Wrocław

61320491R00087